Benjamin Rabbit

by Terry Dinning

Illustrated by Angela Mills

Brimax • Newmarket • England

Benjamin Rabbit is very busy. He and his friends are going to the beach for a picnic, and he is helping to fill the baskets. Mr Rabbit is making lots of sandwiches, while Mrs Rabbit is icing a cake. There are cookies, pies and lemonade. The kitchen is full as everyone helps.

Suddenly they hear a "Toot-toot!" outside. It is Mr Bear, Billy Bear's uncle, the train driver. He is taking everyone to the beach in his little steam train. "Come along!" he calls. Benjamin's friends are already on the train. Freddy Fox, Billy Bear, Wilbur Weasel, Daisy Dormouse and Desmond Duck are all waiting.

"Wait for me!" cries Benjamin. He runs up with the bulging basket. Mr Bear helps him and the basket onto the train.
"Off we go," says Mr Bear. The little train puffs along in the sunshine. Benjamin is sure that this is going to be a special day. The train soon arrives at the beach. "Here we are," says Mr Bear. "Everybody out!"

The sky is blue and the sea is calm.
The sand is golden and warm.
Benjamin jumps out of the train and
pulls off his shoes and his socks.
The sand is soft between his toes.
"I will race you down to the sea," he
calls to his friends, and off they
go. Freddy Fox is the winner.

The waves rush up the sand to meet them, and Benjamin's toes get wet. "The sea is chasing me," he laughs. They all splash about happily in the water.

Mr Bear is setting out the picnic. "Time for lunch," he calls. Everyone is very hungry. They eat the sandwiches, cake and cookies.

"More lemonade, please," says Benjamin.

"Pass the cookies, please," says Wilbur.

When they have finished, they are all too full to run around anymore!

"Oh, my tummy!" says Freddy. "What shall we do now?"

"Now we can build a sandcastle," says Benjamin. They decide to make the biggest sandcastle anyone has ever seen.
"We can put all these shells and stones on the sandcastle,"
says Freddy. Everyone sets to work. The castle grows and grows.

Benjamin goes for a walk along the sand with Daisy and Desmond. They find a sparkling rock pool.
In the pool they find a starfish and a jelly fish, and long ribbons of seaweed. Benjamin finds lots of shells and smooth, shiny stones. He takes them back to show the others.

Then Benjamin hears a tiny voice calling. It is coming from the sea. "Hello," says the voice.
He goes to see who is there. Swimming about in the waves he sees – a little mermaid! Her eyes are as blue as the sea. Her hair is as golden as the sand. She has a fish's tail instead of legs. "Hello," says Benjamin.

"Can you help me, please?" says the little mermaid. "I have lost the big blue stone from my new necklace. The sea has taken it and left it on the beach. Can you find it for me?" "We will all look for it," says Benjamin. He tells his friends about the little mermaid's lost stone and everyone starts to search.

They all find something. Daisy finds a starfish. Billy finds a shell. Wilbur finds a crab. Freddy finds some seaweed. Desmond finds a pebble. But no-one can find the mermaid's lost stone.

"Oh dear," says Benjamin. "We have looked everywhere. Where can it be?" Then he sees something shining on the very top of the sandcastle. He has a closer look.

"Here is your stone, little mermaid," he cries. There is the blue stone. It was on top of the sandcastle the whole time.
"The little mermaid is very happy to have her blue stone back.
"Thank you," she says. "Now I will give you something." She gives Benjamin a great big sea shell.

"Put it up to your ear," she says. Benjamin puts the shell to his ear. "I can hear the sea," he says in surprise. "Yes," smiles the little mermaid. "Now you will always be able to hear the sea, wherever you are."

On the way home, Benjamin listens to the sea in the shell. He will never forget his special day at the beach.

Say these words again.

picnic	ribbons
sandwiches	around
kitchen	voice
sunshine	instead
golden	blue
special	surprise
sparkling	beach